100 WRITING PROMPTS INSPIRED BY SOCIAL MEDIA

By Rekaya Gibson

100 Writing Prompts Inspired by Social Media

By Rekaya Gibson

Gibson Girl Publishing Company, LLC
P. O. Box 11203
Newport News, VA 23601
www.gibsongirlpublishingcompany.com

Cover Design: Rekaya Gibson
Cover Photo: Canva.com

ISBN: 978-1976801983

Printed in the United States

Table of Contents

Introduction

I'm excited to share *100 Writing Prompts Inspired by Social Media* with you. I spend hours on social media each day, and I am often captivated by what I see. It could be a status, video, or meme that triggers my writing genie. I have decided to compile my endless thoughts into one document, in hopes of sparking creativity in others. Let's get started writing!

What to Expect

Some prompts don't require much time, while others take longer. I give scenarios and sentences to jump-start the process. Some you can use as warm-up exercises, and others as a workshop or classroom assignment. Also, I provide insight into certain words to give greater understanding.

How to Use this Book

- Choose the specific topic you desire. (You don't have to start at the beginning.)
- Free writing–writing without stopping to correct spelling and grammar
- Enjoy reading what you wrote.

Resource Bonus

I've included a list of resources that have been useful throughout my writing journey. It contains some of my favorite books, websites, and much more to keep you writing.

I hope you will find the contents of this eBook useful. If so, please leave a review, tell a friend, or share with your network. Thank you.

Happy Writing!

Rekaya Gibson

1. Start your story with these three words: *I remember when...*

2. Write a direct message to the woman who keeps sending nude pictures to your deceased spouse on social media. The spouse died three days ago, after choking on a hot dog.

3. Five people volunteered to help plan your cousin Vinny's birthday party. They included Vinny's friends: The Gooch, a local tavern owner; The Hammer, the neighborhood watchman; Lady Lorraine, Vinny's mom and retired school teacher; Mini-Myra, Vinny's neighbor and city councilperson; and lastly, Gypsy Gold, Vinny's girlfriend of 20 years. Write character profiles for each. A character profile can include, but is not limited to, the following: physical characteristics, personality traits, mannerisms, likes or dislikes, and details about their past.

4. Write a dating profile description for *Meet Me at the Altar Dating Services*.

5. A foul smell keeps coming from your daughter's room, so you decide to clean it up. You look under her bed and discover a dead man. She catches you and asks if you could help her dispose of the evidence. You agree. Tell the rest of the story.

6. Write a product review of something known to give customers diarrhea. You caught a case and can't wait to put the company on blast.

7. Think of a scent that reminds you of a moment in time. Now, tell a story about it using the five Ws (Who, What, When, Where, Why).

8. Write a 'Thank You' letter to a historical figure you admire.

9. Using your zodiac sign, write a 150-word horoscope for the daily newspaper.

10. The lights flickered before shutting off permanently, due to tropical storm Hermes. To entertain three six-year-old children, Ms. Margaret tells them a ghost story. Write a ghost story for the children. Keep it brief and scary.

11. Today, Molly goes to preschool. Her stay-at-home mom gets her there early to become acquainted with the teacher and the classroom. When it's time for parents to leave, Molly informs her mom she wants to go home too. Unfortunately, she must stay. Explain to Molly the importance of staying at school on her first day.

12. You're forced to leave the country. You have 10
minutes to gather your personal items. What do you take?
What do you say to your family and friends?

13. "My Country, 'Tis of Thee", also known as "America", is an American patriotic song written by Samuel Francis Smith. The lyrics can be found on the National Institutes of Health website here: https://kids.niehs.nih.gov/games/songs/patriotic/my-country-tis-of-thee. Write your own version of the song.

14. You finished your first 5K (3.1 miles) race. Describe how it feels to a 97-year-old former track star who is now blind.

15. Your cat, Abby Kitty, is sick. The only things that make her feel better are being held and you singing. Make up a song to sing to Abby Kitty.

16. Write a 50-word synopsis or summary of your life.

17. If you were transported to the setting of the last movie you watched, where would you be? Now, describe it in detail. (Setting includes time and geographic location. It can also include culture, historical period, geography, and hour.)

18. Write a movie review for one of your favorite movies.

19. List seven things you learned in kindergarten. How do they still apply to your life today?

20. You just learned via text message that you became the President of the United States. Write an acceptance speech to unify the country without using the words *come together*.

21. A woman catches her husband sleeping with the pastor. The pastor flees the hotel room naked, and the wife goes to her car to retrieve a gun. The husband calls 9-1-1. Write the dialog between the husband and the 9-1-1 operator.

22. Write your obituary. Announce the death by beginning with your name, age, and place of residence. Also, include the time and place of death. List those predeceased as well as the surviving loved ones' names. Then, write biographical information such as schools attended, place of employment, organization memberships, and hobbies or special interests. Conclude with the service times and a special message.

23. The great debate over which one hurts worst: a Brazilian wax (all hair removed from genital area) or childbirth. Pick a side. Write your response, which includes an introduction, your main point(s) and supporting evidence, and finally, a conclusion. Neither topic applies to you? It's fiction, go for it!

24. You own an ant farm, and the ants started a church of worship. Discuss the church's structure, membership requirements, and when and where services are held.

25. Rewrite your favorite childhood fairytale. Create the story for ages one to three; limit it to 500 words.

26. Write a story using this opening line: *I love the way the air smells right before it starts to rain.*

27. Create a fake news headline <u>and</u> story from a fake news network. Don't forget the five Ws (Who, What, When, Where, Why) and How.

28. You are 16 years old again. Write an open letter to your
mother. An open letter is sometimes critical and intended
for public viewing.

29. You're an English professor at Blue Bayou Community College. Explain alternative facts to your students and share three examples.

30. Valentine's Day is upon us. You purchased a gift for the homeless man you pass on the street every day. What do you buy him? Now, write a gift message that gives him hope.

31. Create a book or short story title for each word:
- Danger
- Table
- Indigo
- Microphone
- Angel
- Caliber
- Value
- Moon pies
- Caboose
- Ferrari
- Aftermath

For example: *Danger Comes in the Morning* - Feel free to use that one.

32. Your blog offers sponsored advertisement for businesses to promote their products. Name your blog, write its mission, and describe your target audience.

33. *Underwrite the Cause* is an online platform which allows individuals, groups, and organizations to raise money for life events and causes. Select your event or cause, and then write a story that convinces people to donate.

34. Create a chain letter consisting of a threat of bad luck if the recipients don't adhere to the conditions. Don't forget to instruct social media friends to copy and paste the chain letter to their page.

35. Think about something you have cooked. Now, write the recipe. Include the ingredients and instructions. For non-cooks, microwave cooking and reheating count for this one.

36. You've owned a restaurant for over 45 years at the same location. You plan to close it down in 30 days. Write a letter to your loyal customers, informing them of your decision.

37. The state trooper adjusted his bodycam as he approached the red sports car.

"Do you know how fast you were driving?" he asked the gentleman behind the wheel.

"No sir," Miles replied.

"You were driving 55 in a 45-speed zone."

Miles nodded in agreement and handed the trooper his paperwork.

What happened next makes news headlines nationwide and becomes subject of multiple debates on social media.

Complete the story.

38. "You Explain It Challenge!" Write instructions to the next social media challenge. Don't forget to name it. A social media challenge is a game, dance, song, or image that individuals copy and post on social media, using the same hashtag. Some of the most popular challenges have been the ALS Ice Bucket, the Harlem Shake, and the Running Man.

39. While walking in the rose garden at the Metropolitan Menagerie, Bonnie overhears Saint Francis talking to the birds about the first bloom. Write his sermon.

40. Describe your greatest accomplishment without using adverbs. Include when it happened, how you felt, and share any challenges, limitations, and/or setbacks. Explain why it was worth it or if you have any regrets.

41. List ten reasons to bring back granny-panties. Granny-panties are underwear that fully cover the buttocks with sides that extend below the hip.

42. Every day is a national food holiday in the United States. Create your own national food, cultural, or religious holiday. Describe its origin and traditions, include a date, suggest ways to celebrate, and mention anything else that makes your holiday special.

43. You partied all night with your pals and you haven't slept for 27 hours. Before heading home, you stop at the city government building to handle some personal business. When you enter the elevator, you notice three elderly women, two non-confirmed meth users, and a uniformed police officer. The elevator gets stuck between floors six and seven. A maintenance worker informs the group that it will take about an hour to get things moving again. Begin your story here.

44. You have served in the military for 35 years and plan to retire in five years, at the age of 60. You will live off the interest from your inheritance and use your pension for something else. Discuss your retirement plans.

45. "I can't stand wearing high heels; I tower over the clouds." Build an imaginary world using this concept.

46. Melanie lost 11 pounds in seven days on the Watermelon Diet. Now, she helps others to realize their dream. Create a seven-day menu that Melanie can share with her social media friends. Include three meals and two snacks per day.

47. Write lyrics to a song using the following chorus: *Black beans, candied yams, cornbread, and baked chicken.*

48. Write seven motivational quotes to add to your social media page, one for each day of the week. Use one word in each quote: water, business, shoelaces, balloon, podcast, tie, and cake.

49. In 165 characters, write a story about a girl and her
dinosaur.

50. Water symbolizes many things. Explain what role water plays in your life and what it signifies.

51. Select a teacher you had in school or your child's
teacher. Write a letter to the school board on the
individual's behalf, advocating for a pay raise.

52. During a Louisiana swamp tour, three people fall into the murky water. They struggle to stay afloat. You can only save one: your best friend, a five-year-old or your favorite politician. Explain to the news reporter who you saved, why, and how.

53. You've just won a million dollars (after taxes) in the
Nevada Lottery. Describe your reaction, how this makes
you feel, and the impact it will have on your life.

54. Mack Montgomery removed the fur from the possum and drained the blood from its neck. Then, he cut the tail and pulled back the hide. He made an incision around the anus, put his hands inside the animal's stomach, and removed its organs. Mack used a sharp knife for the decapitation. He rinsed water over the possum's body to clean it. Aunt Greta entered the kitchen to watch the ritual. She insisted that a raccoon is a cleaner animal than a possum. Give her explanation as to why.

55. Write a birthday card to someone special. What would it read on the outside? What would it read on the inside?

56. Colin's neighbor keeps to herself. She doesn't speak or wave in the mornings when he leaves for work. He never sees anyone visit the home and her car never moves from the driveway. Every night at eleven thirty, blue holiday lights illuminate the garage and Colin hears a buzz saw. One night, Colin watered his lawn at the same time as the neighbor's nightly activity. He approached her home and opened the side door to the garage. Describe what Colin witnessed, her reaction when she noticed him, and what Colin did next.

57. A dead blackbird was found on the ground near the train's platform with its shattered wing pointing to the sky. A baseball was on the ground, three feet away. Tell a story about what happened.

58. Identify three black objects in your current environment. Link the three to tell a story. Write for 15 minutes. Don't forget to set a timer.

59. When cows and termites fart, they release methane gas into the atmosphere, contributing to global warming. Create a story with an alternate world where cows and termites don't exist.

60. Every episode of Three's Company, a '70's television sitcom, included a misunderstanding and resolution. Read the sentence below.

"I can't go shopping with you today; I'm waiting on the weed man," Camille overheard her mother tell someone on the telephone.

Now, use the sentence to write a 1,500-word story as a misunderstanding. Don't forget to resolve the conflict.

61. Sherman paddles his boat down the Santee River, looking for the Sewee Indian Tribe. They live and trade goods along the South Carolina riverbanks. Sherman's children reside with the elders, and he hopes to find them. He spots a flag, which he recalls belonging to the tribe. Use your creativity to describe the flag of the Sewee Indian Tribe. Include tribal colors, symbols, and their meanings.

62. A cafe sign reads: *Patrons come here to partake in our delicious teas and to enjoy their kid-free time away from home. If your little Becky screams and scrubs the floor with her Cute Patrol outfit for more than three minutes, you must…*
Complete the sentence with at least five rules for parents to follow.

63. The presidential dogs reside in the White House until their expiration date. Sable, a golden retriever, has lived through two presidencies. She rarely left the room when important discussions took place. Summer Reign, an author-friend, convinced Sable to tell her story about serving the two presidents, one from each party. The Democrats and the Republicans begged Sable not to write her memoirs. She couldn't commit to an entire book, but she managed to share something about President Barack Obama and President Donald Trump. Write Sable's deathbed confessions in 250-words.

64. Seventy-eight-year-old Abigail Carter received 27 marriage proposals that she never accepted. She felt she'd never met the right man at the right time or place. Write a marriage proposal that would convince her to say yes.

65. Hammer Helmet, a popular streaming service, is making original films. Screenwriters can submit their movie scripts on the company's website. Hammer Helmet prefers dysfunctional characters – the crazier the better. Keeping this in mind, pitch a film idea using a logline. A logline is a one- or two-sentence summary of a film. It includes the hook and/or central conflict. *Example: Two teenagers from rival families fall in love and, without knowing, cause each other's death.*

66. Six years ago, Edward was living in his car. He got behind on his bills, and his house went into foreclosure. His food truck business failed and so did his marriage. He felt humiliated and depressed all the time. He couldn't believe that he once worked at an oil company with a six-figure salary. Now, Ed owns a condo and thriving fitness and wellness center with his fiancé. His family and friends cannot believe his transformation. What changed for Ed? Write his testimonial.

67. According to the Merriam-Webster dictionary, shenanigans mean devious tricks used especially for an underhanded purpose or a mischievous activity. Think about a time you engaged in shenanigans. Now, tell the story.

68. Molly and Greg were madly in love when they were 23.
Molly got pregnant with her third baby girl, Colleen. Molly
and Greg gave Colleen up for adoption before the state
could take her away. Now, at the age of 44, Molly and
Greg are married, and they have twin boys, age 16. Though
Molly and Greg lived in the same town as the girls, they
would never acknowledge them on the street. Colleen plans
to leave for the Army soon. Molly writes Colleen a letter to
explain the custody issue. She also apologizes for giving
her away. What does the letter say?

69. Maurice stood in line, like most Americans, to get the flu shot. Neighborhood pharmacies offered them for free since universal healthcare passed in 2025. Maurice never bothered getting one. He'd heard stories about people getting sick afterwards. The injection also caused bruising at the injection point. This year, the president urged everyone to get the medicine because of a deadly flu strain. A whopping 349 people had died, and the number increased every day. Groutmen, a domestic terrorist group, accepted responsibility for the deaths and bragged, "This is only the beginning," on national social media. The government asked people not to panic; there was no proof the group was spreading the virus. Maurice stepped up to the nurses' station for his turn. "I'm sorry, sir; I have administered the last dose. The next shipment won't come in until next month," Nurse Judy replied. Start your story with his response.

70. Choose a superhero power: invisibility, speed runner, or the ability to fly. You have ten minutes to use the power to save the world. Write a story about the sudden-death situation. Don't forget to set your clock. Humanity is counting on you.

71. If you hold your index finger in the air, it can transport
you to another realm. Think about where you would like to
be right now. Describe what you see; who is there with
you, if anyone; and what you are doing.

72. People love using the proverbial phrase, "When life
gives you lemons, make lemonade." It means, when facing
adversity, use it to your advantage to come out on top.
Think about a time when life threw you lemons. Write
about it and discuss how you made lemonade. Cheers!

73. I've decided to boil my husband for Father's Day. He died last night, and I have no place to put the body. His stale flesh will enhance the gumbo that I'm making in his honor. The children were looking forward to spending time with him. I cannot think of a better way. Write a passage surrounding the circumstances of the husband's death.

74. Your best friends are marrying each other on Saturday. They have asked you to give a three-minute speech at the reception. They have one requirement: don't mention the past. Write a speech of 389 words.

75. Everyone has at least one prized possession. List your favorite three. Think about how they are they related and different. Create a 1,000-word story that includes all three.

76. Nathaniel pulled into his driveway. He observed a golden retriever surveying the bushes next to his house. He didn't recognize the dog, but tags dangled from its neck. Nathaniel approached in a calm, friendly manner. The animal wagged his tail with delight. Both greeted each other like old pals. "Hi Neighbor," a baritone voice came from the shrubs. Nathaniel separated the leaves to find a man squatting and defecating on his property. Continue writing the story.

77. Your devilish side came out to play today. Give it a name and place it on your left shoulder. Set the scene. Now, what's your devil saying to you? If you need reinforcements, it's okay to call the devil's archenemy: Angel Delight.

78. You agreed to write an infomercial for Butt-Her-Love,
a daily moisturizer for the body. Annabelle maintains a
round, soft derriere by using the product. She loves the
results. Write an ad for this product.

79. Find a picture or image from social media, your
personal computer, your phone, your house, or wherever
you are now. Study it. Tell a story about what you see.

80. Look at the calendar and the clock. Jot down the date and the time. Where is your character right now? What is he or she doing? Who is with your character? What is your character saying?

81. So, you want to write a book and don't know how to
get started. Write or type everything you want to say about
the story. Keep writing. No editing and researching. Get it
on paper. If you're writing fiction, start with the scene
that's fresh on your mind right now or you have thought
about in the past. If you're writing nonfiction, start writing
the information that resonates with you right now.

82. Ask yourself, "Why is it important that I write this book?" Write your answer. Get everything off your chest. It might begin to sound like an introduction to a nonfiction book. Or, it might help explain to others why you want to write.

83. Go outdoors or look out a window. Find two images in nature. How are they connected? Now, write a three-line haiku poem about nature with 17 syllables: first line with five, second line with seven, and third line with five. Do not title the poem.

84. Think about how you want to end your novel or short story. Now, write the ending. It's okay to start with the ending.

85. Write dialogue between a fiction and nonfiction character. To help you get started, begin with this: *You're doing it wrong; can't you drive straight?*

86. Write down five goals you can achieve in the next three months. Goals are specific, measurable, achievable, realistic, and timely. For example, my goal is to lose ten pounds in three months.

87. Use the first letter of your last name to create a list of five words. Use the first letter of your birth month to create five more words. Tell a story using all ten words. Limit yourself to one paragraph. Yes, it must make sense.

88. Lucy has found a cure for cancer, but she refuses to share it with her archenemy, Ambernostre, who is dying from the disease. Lucy claims she seeks revenge because of the ridicules and insults received on social media. This upset her business partner, Craven, and he left the firm. He is the only other person who knows where to find the medicine. Lucy stores the antidote somewhere on a private island in the South Pacific. She retrieves it when necessary and brings it to the mainland. Then, she contacts the on-call physician to administer the drug using a port, a medical device installed beneath the skin. Help save Ambernostre's life. Get her that drug by developing a plan to accomplish this mission.

89. Your spouse discovers your unfinished memoir in the home safe. You had intended to complete it and send it to a New York agent; however, you died last month from biting your tongue, which became infected with gangrene. Now, your partner sits in the living room reading the opening line to your life. What is written?

90. How would you prefer a novel or story to end? Write an alternative ending to a novel or story. Can't think of anything? Use movie or a television show. Remember, endings can be happy or sad, contain a twist, or be left open-ended.

91. Think about something you lost. Write down the details surrounding its disappearance. Also, answer informative questions such as: What was it? What did it mean to you? How did it make you feel when you had it? How does it make you feel now that it's gone? What have you done to fill the void? What can replace it?

92. In 1971, Mona, a single woman who worked as a secretary, applied for a credit card with Century Liberty Bank. The company sent her a polite letter declining her application because of her marital status. Write the letter.

93. Grady hides socks and avocado pits around the house. When his dad isn't looking, Grady removes the batteries from the television remotes. Write his explanation as to why he is doing these things and what he is doing with the items.

94. Rewrite slogans or taglines to five brands that you like or dislike. Example: *Sandpaper, a wardrobe collection that goes beyond pretty.*

95. Women in this country have gone mad. They have
rescinded their church memberships, removed and burned
their bras again, and stopped cooking. Last month, they met
at the nation's capital for a rally. Who spoke and what was
said to get these ladies riled up?

96. Nolan accidentally rode his urban bike into a $90,000 car parked on the street. It damaged the passenger-side door. Nolan writes an apology letter to the owner. What does it say?

97. Nadine Liverpool would love to work for Mrs. Parsons, owner of Cow Tongue Chips, located in Abnerville, North Dakota. The company makes cow tongue potato chips in five flavors. Nadine prepared her resume, but she needs help with the career profile section. Write it for her, in paragraph form. A career profile is a summary of skills and expertise.

98. Write a letter to your younger self. Include details about the setting. Also, reveal something about yourself so that readers can identify the era.

99. Nia has been in a ten-year on-again, off-again
relationship with George. Each date ended with drama. Last
month, both admitted their faults and made amends;
however, their toxic relationship took a turn for the worse
and they called it quits for good. Give us the juicy details
surrounding the most recent breakup.

100. Karma Doesn't Live Here Anymore is a stage play written by comedian Lance Soto Romero. Write the plot, the main events of the play. Make it funny!

Bonus: Write a goodbye message to social media. Explain why you no longer want to use it as a form of communication with friends and family. Don't forget to let people know you will be deleting your account.

Conclusion

Congratulations! You made it through *100 Writing Prompts Inspired by Social Media*. I hope you have enjoyed the experience and created some awesome content. Want more resources? Check out the list on the next pages. If you need further assistance, feel free to contact me regarding a one-on-one consultation. I offer coaching services to help you finish and publish your book and/or launch your freelance writing career. I have provided my contact information on the last page. I wish you continued success. Thanks again!

RESOURCES

<u>Books</u>

Formatting & Submitting Your Manuscript 2nd Edition (2004)
by Editors of Writer's Digest Books
This book features both good and bad sample submissions for manuscripts, query letters, proposals, cover letters, outlines, synopses, and more. In addition, you'll find information on specific genres and electronic submissions.

Writer's Market 2017: The Most Trusted Guide to Getting Published 96th Edition (2016)
by Robert Lee Brewer
This guide takes you through the process of getting published and paid for your writing by offering thousands of publishing opportunities, including listings for book publishers, consumer and trade magazines, contests and awards, and literary agents.

Building Online Relationships: One Reader at a Time (2015)
by LaShaunda Hoffman
This how-to guide helps authors to promote like a pro and build trust with readers, so they become loyal buyers. Each chapter includes an action plan you can implement immediately.

<u>Websites</u>

FundsforWriters.com
This is an online resource for writers looking for funding. It includes grant opportunities, contests, markets, publishers, agents, and jobs. www.fundsforwriters.com

Jane Friedman
With more than 20 years of experience in the business of publishing and media, she can help you make smart decisions about your publishing and digital media strategy, and position you for long-term growth.
www.janefriedman.com

Make a Living Writing
Blogger Carol Trice has practical advice and resources for writers, offers one-on-one mentoring, and teaches Article Writing Masterclass, Pitch Clinic, and 4-Week Journalism School. www.makealivingwriting.com

<u>Much More</u>

Blogger to Author Podcast
This podcast helps content creators get inspired and motivated to write and publish their books. Explains how bloggers or entrepreneurs are using their books to grow their businesses. www.bloggertoauthor.com

Poets & Writers Magazine
The publication contains essays on the literary life,
practical guidance for getting published and pursuing
writing careers, in-depth profiles of poets, fiction writers,
and writers of creative nonfiction, and conversation among
fellow professionals. It also, provides a comprehensive
listing of literary grants and awards, deadlines, and
prizewinners available in print. www.pw.org

Rasilliant Enterprises
This business provides professional editing, writing
services, and content solutions.
www.rasilliantenterprises.com

ABOUT AUTHOR REKAYA GIBSON

As a freelance writer for more than 10 years, Rekaya Gibson, MPA, has written content for Amtrak, Writer's Digest Books, and various lifestyle magazines. Currently, she writes full-time and maintains a food blog based on her novel, *The Food Temptress*. She also contributes monthly content to *Cuisine Noir Magazine*. She has authored six other books in various genres as well. When she isn't scribing, Rekaya is talking sports on her weekly podcast, Black Girls Talk Sports, or exploring Virginia's 200+ wineries. Learn more about Ms. Gibson here: www.RekayaGibson.com. If you need to reach her directly, email: Rekaya@RekayaGibson.com

Connect with Rekaya on Social Media
LinkedIn: RekayaGibson
Twitter: @RekayaGibson
Facebook: www.facebook.com/AuthorRekayaGibson
Instagram: the_food_temptress

Pick Up Other Titles by This Author
(Available worldwide where books are sold or request them at your local library)

Cooking on a Dollar Store Budget (Cookbook)
eBook and Paperback

The Food Temptress (Magical Realism)
eBook and Paperback

Continue on Next Page
Mama Don't Like Ugly (Contemporary /Young Adult)
Audio Book, eBook, and Paperback

Are There French Fries in Heaven? (Children's
Book/Christian)
eBook and Paperback

My Mama's Sweet Potato Pie/El Pay de Camote di mi
Mama: A Coloring Book (Children's Book)
Paperback